Animals in the Hot Desert

Katie Peters

GRL Consultants,
Diane Craig and Monica Marx,
Certified Literacy Specialists

Pull Ahead Readers

Lerner Publications ◆ Minneapolis

Note from a GRL Consultant
This Pull Ahead leveled book has been carefully designed for beginning readers. A team of guided reading literacy experts has reviewed and leveled the book to ensure readers pull ahead and experience success.

Lerner Publications Company
A division of Lerner Publishing Group, Inc.
241 First Avenue North
Minneapolis, MN 55401 USA

For reading levels and more information, look up this title at www.lernerbooks.com.

Main body text set in Memphis Pro 24/39
Typeface provided by Linotype.

Photo Acknowledgments
The images in this book are used with the permission of: © iStockphoto, 3, 4–5, 6–7, 8–9, 10–11, 12–13, 16 (top left, top middle, top right, bottom right, bottom left); © Shutterstock, 14–15, 16 (bottom middle)

Front cover: © iStockphoto

Library of Congress Cataloging-in-Publication Data

Names: Peters, Katie, author.
Title: Animals in the hot desert / Katie Peters.
Description: Minneapolis : Lerner Publications, [2020] | Series: Let's look at animal habitats (Pull ahead readers - Nonfiction) | Includes index. | Audience: Age 4–7. | Audience: K to Grade 3.
Identifiers: LCCN 2018059821 (print) | LCCN 2019000028 (ebook) | ISBN 9781541562011 (eb pdf) | ISBN 9781541558618 (lb : alk. paper) | ISBN 9781541573109 (pb : alk. paper)
Subjects: LCSH: Desert animals—Juvenile literature.
Classification: LCC QL116 (ebook) | LCC QL116 .P46 2020 (print) | DDC 591.754—dc23

LC record available at https://lccn.loc.gov/2018059821

Manufactured in the United States of America
2-51147-46242-6/8/2021

Contents

Animals in the Hot Desert

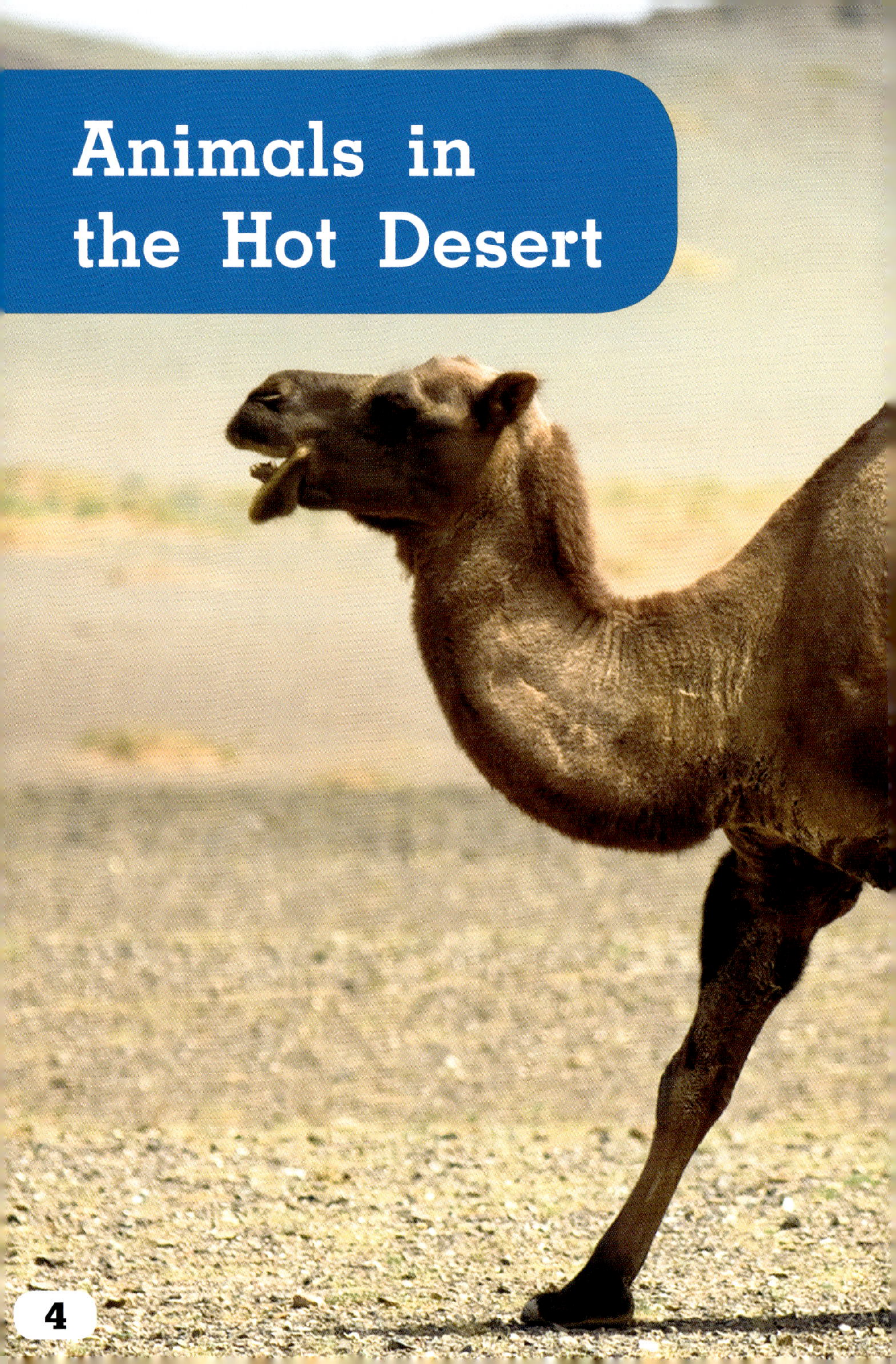

The camel is in the desert.
The camel is tall.

The lizard is in the desert.
The lizard is on a rock.

The owl is in the desert.
The owl is on a cactus.

The tortoise is in the desert.

The tortoise is slow.

The snake is in the desert.

The snake is long.

The spider is in the desert.
The spider is hairy.

Did You See It?

camel

lizard

owl

snake

spider

tortoise

Index